Copyright © 2025 Jennifer Jones
All copyright laws and rights reserved.
Published in the U.S.A.
For more information, email info@ninjalifehacks.tv
Paperback ISBN: 978-1-63731-936-9
Hardcover ISBN: 978-1-63731-938-3
eBook ISBN: 978-1-63731-937-6

Find the Crayon Hospital lesson plans at ninjalifehacks.tv

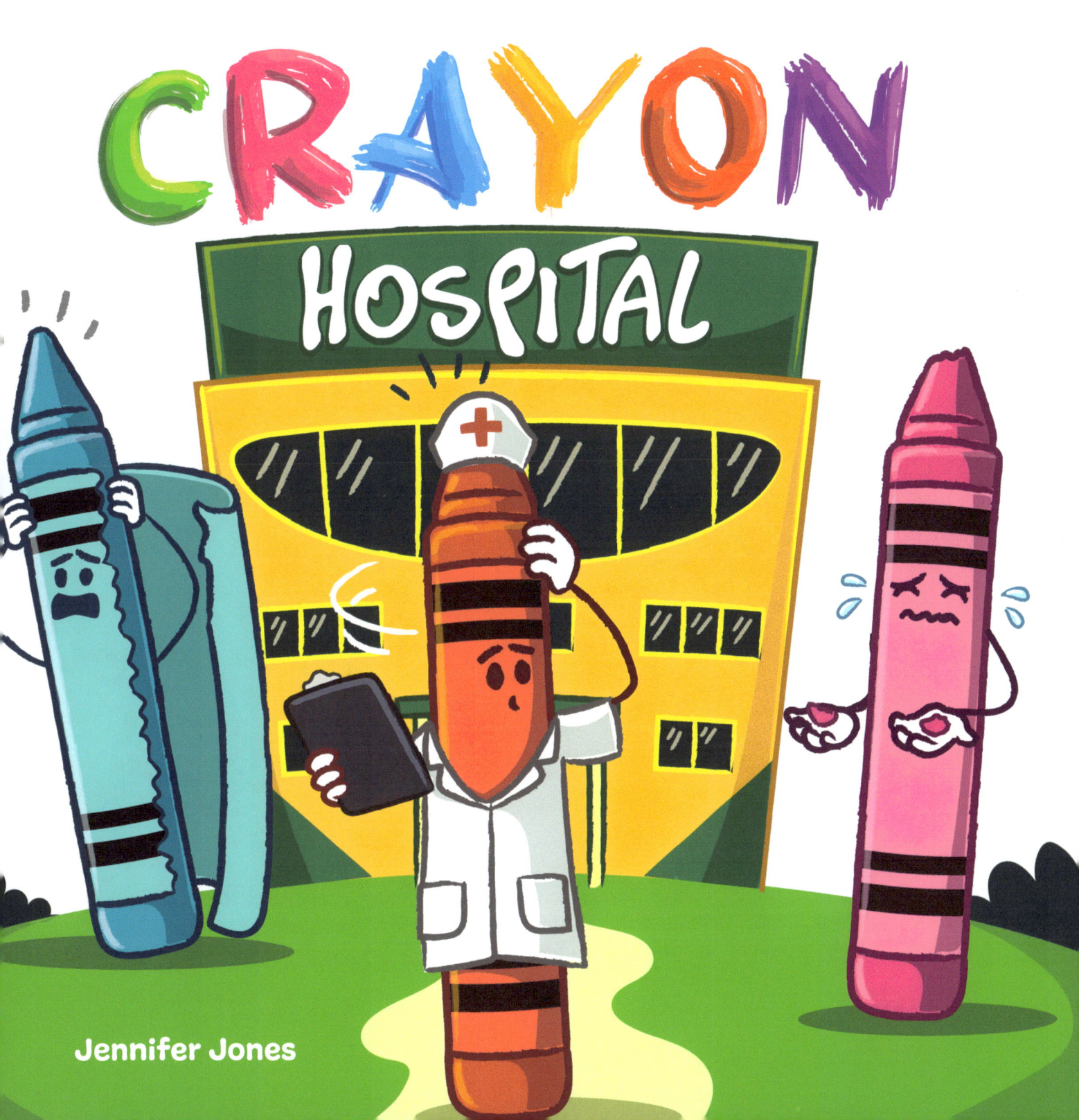

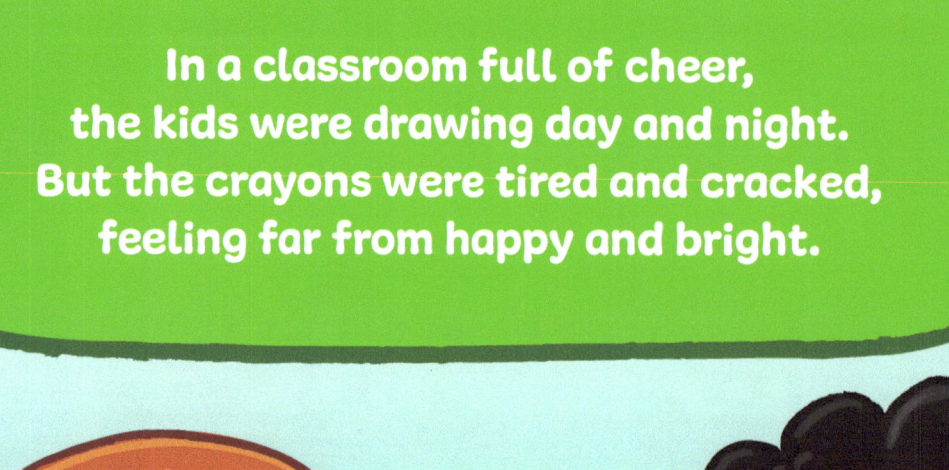

In a classroom full of cheer,
the kids were drawing day and night.
But the crayons were tired and cracked,
feeling far from happy and bright.

They snapped them in two without a thought
and peeled their wrappers clean away.
The crayons sighed, "We've had enough!"
Their vibrant hues began to fade.

Meanwhile, back in class, the kids noticed something wasn't right. Their crayon box was empty now, and the guilt began to bite.

"Dear Crayons," one child wrote with care.
"We're sorry for all the stress we caused.
We promise now to treat you well
and keep your colors bold and strong."

Another child drew bright flowers
with crayons that were left behind.
"We miss you, Crayons! Please come back.
We've got new pictures on our mind."

So if you have a crayon box, be gentle, treat them as your friends. Or else they might just take a trip to Crayon Hospital to make amends!

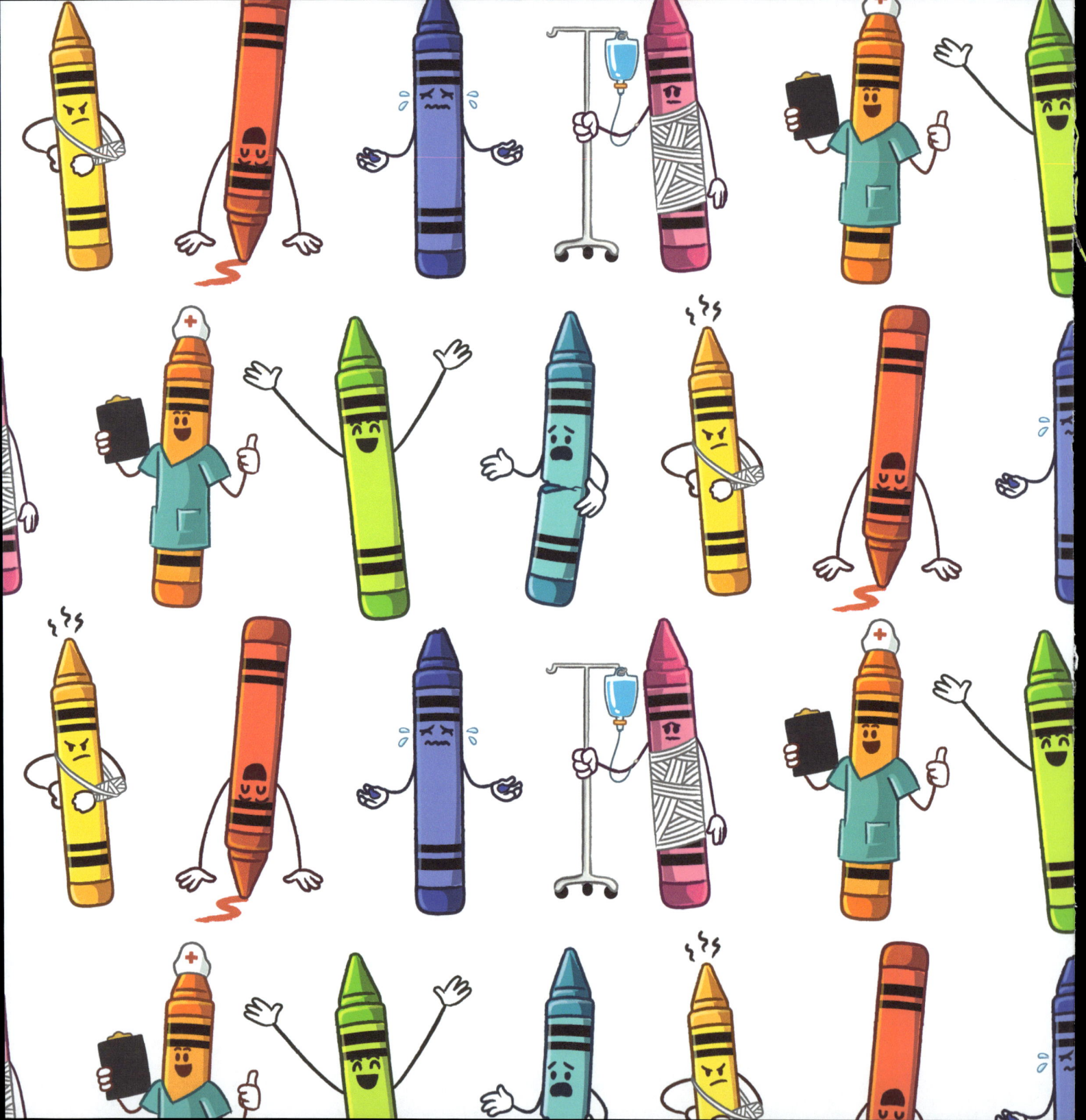

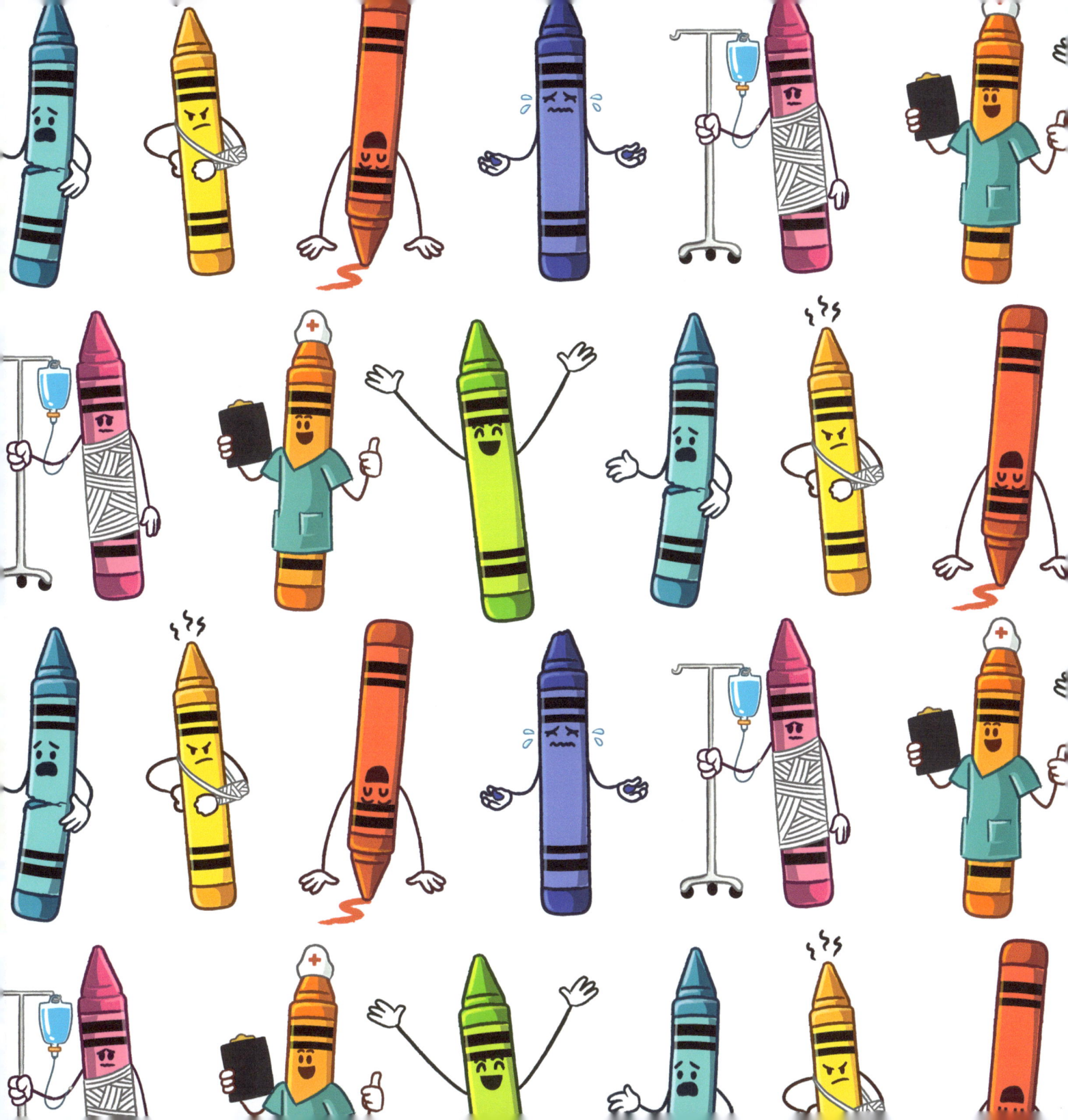

www.ingramcontent.com/pod-product-compliance
Lightning Source LLC
Chambersburg PA
CBHW041711160426
43209CB00018B/1799